Autumn Sun
The Bright Side of Aging

Autumn Sun

The Bright Side of Aging

by
Genevieve Smith Whitford

For information about permission to reproduce
selections from this book, write to Permissions,
Harp Press, c/o Kaleidoscope Publishing,
295 E. Swedesford Road, #121, Wayne, Pennsylvania 19087.

Publisher's Cataloging-in-Publication
(Provided by Quality Books, Inc.)

Whitford, Genevieve Smith.
   Autumn sun : the bright side of aging / by Genevieve
Smith Whitford. – 1st ed.
   p. cm.
   LCCN 2002109974
   ISBN 0-9706593-8-5

   1. Aging–Poetry.   I. Title

PS3573.H492A98 2002   811'.54
                    QBI02-701893

Cover and book design:
Jennica A. Musselman

Cover art:
Autumn Solitude © Peter Ellenshaw. By arrangement with
Mill Pond Press, Inc. Venice, FL 34292. For information
on the limited edition prints by Peter Ellenshaw,
contact Mill Pond Press at 1-800-535-0331.

Leaf illustrations:
Patricia Stokes

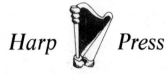

Harp *Press*

201 W. Evergreen Avenue, #904
Philadelphia, Pennsylvania 19118
Telephone: 215.248.9860
E-mail: KScopePub@aol.com
Website: www.genevievewhitford.com
Please address or call the above for ordering information.

Also by Genevieve Smith Whitford:

Queen Anne's Lace

The Sound of the Harp

*To the thoughtful, loving children
and the spirited, caring friends
who make late life a blessing.*

Acknowledgements

Thank you to Charles and Joan Adelman, Caroline Baldi, Faith Bustard, Eugene and Edith Fertman, Jean Folger, Alba Hyk, Marian Sitarchuk, and Deborah Ward for their editorial comments, proofreading skills, and encouragement.

To Patricia Stokes for her sense of line and color and the sketches of leaves throughout the book.

And to Betsy Quinn and Bruce Montgomery for their interest in providing an appropriate and colorful cover for *Autumn Sun.*

Foreword

For the fiftieth reunion of our class from Northwestern University, we were asked to write a one-page letter about what we'd been doing for the past fifty years. Adelaide Boyd Davis spoke for all of us when she said, "If autobiographies must be written, what a time in our lives to write one – these mornings when we rise with strong feelings of well-being, when we watch so many things come full circle and when we have learned to like ourselves . . .

" . . . As I move back through the years today I realize that in the end we all write the same biography. We all have struggled along, learning what we needed to learn. We coped, we grew, shaped by individual experiences. Few things happened that we were prepared for. Finally we all discovered the same truths."

The most surprising truth I have discovered is that the late years can be the best time of your life. You feel strong and confident as never before and you are free at last to be yourself. Growing up in the Depression, surviving a war, acquiring an education, finding a career, and raising a family are no small feats. We wonder how we did it. Would anyone want to start all over again? When you've spent a lifetime wondering where you're going, isn't it a relief to know where you've been?

Another great surprise is that you feel young inside, whatever your age, and you never stop learning.

When your health fails, you realize that old age is not for sissies, but now you know that you are strong and can cope. You know that you can't win all life's challenges and it doesn't matter. You have nothing more to prove.

I marvel at my peers, who accept their limitations, count their blessings, and take each day as it comes. Growing old has shown me the strength and resilience of the human spirit.

Glory be!

Genevieve Smith Whitford

Autumn Sun

The Bright Side of Aging

In the midst of winter I finally learned
that there is in me an invincible summer.

Albert Camus

Who Am I?

Who am I?
At sixty, I still ask.
First, child of loving parents.
Carry me, Daddy!
I remember saying it
in Christmas rush
on State Street in Chicago
when I was very small,
and he lifted me
and I rested in his arms.

I wailed again
when Mother left the house,
but Daddy said,
Be a good girl
and we will bring you
a baby brother,
and they did.

Babe no more,
I am a sister now.
When I smile
he smiles back at me,
when he cries
I wipe away his tears.
But when I try to hold him
he struggles to be free.

And then he grows
and tortures me.
In innocence,
he blinds my doll
and spoils my game.
I become a bad girl.
How can you be mean
to your very own brother?
says my mother.

And then to school.
I am a painful conscience,
a wonderer.
Where do babies come from?
Who is God?
What does it mean?

In high school
and in college,
I am a student,
but not a scholar,
a harpist,
but not a musician,
an actor,
but not a star,
an editor,
but not a writer,
an also-ran.

I graduate and rush into the arms
of him who says,
You are an angel!
But what do angels know
of getting meals
and scrubbing floors?

You are pregnant,
says the doctor.
I walk home on clouds
and then begin to retch.
I am all body,
resisting,
releasing,
and then becoming
a mother.

She is my all now,
but where am I?
No matter.
No time.
I suckle her, then worry
lest the milk run dry.
I want the best for her,
but where am I?
Lost in diapers
and Little League
and P.T.A.

This too will pass
and we will say good-bye
to graduates
and travelers
and unsuspecting brides.

They are all gone.
Our empty arms
embrace grandchildren now.
But who is this
who teaches them
to Patty Cake
and Peek-a-Boo?
Surely my mother,
or her mother before her.
They are the same songs,
the same gestures,
the same games.
Automatically,
they come from me.

I see it now.
I am a shell.
I grow and calcify.
Cells divide within me,
ideas evolve,
but nothing is permanent,
nothing new . . .

I am a temporary source
of life flow,
of ideas,
of traditions;
a vessel
to contain,
to nurture,
to pour forth.

I dandle the latest baby
on my knee.
Trot, trot to Boston
to buy a loaf of bread.
Trot, trot back again,
the old trot's dead!

Don't cry!
The wine of life flows on,
from yeasty depths
of each succeeding generation,
in quality and color
of infinite variation,
distilled in me,
absorbed by you
in life's brief celebration.

Gray September Day

On a gray September day
we drive away
from our last child,
standing uncertainly
on a strange college campus,
waving good-bye
to his childhood
and his family.
There is a wrench
and rush of tears
as this last cord is cut,
another one of life's connections
broken,
leaving us weakened
and detached.

Now we move in new directions,
following our interests,
developing our talents,
remembering what we were
before we had children,
for now we are all of that
and more.

Autumn Sun

The autumn sun
fills our empty rooms
with warmth and light.
We stretch ourselves,
free to roam and grow,
no longer caught
in the clutter and distraction
of domesticity.
We are strong and confident
as never before,
now that our children are grown
in competence and wisdom
beyond our expectations,
multiplying our hopes,
extending our dreams,
returning our love.
Now there is time
to develop old talents,
to renew old friendships,
to revive old passions,
to discover new interests.
As leaf colors with seeding done,
so may we glow in autumn sun.

Midnight

The minute hand moves,
relentlessly,
toward the midnight
of my sixty-fifth year.
How can I be old
and yet feel young?
I've just begun to live!
I'm still learning how
to run a house,
to cook a meal,
to manage a family,
to control my emotions,
to play the harp,
to write poetry.
Even at this moment,
which startles me
into awareness,
the writing of a poem
seems more important
than the ticking of the clock.

Family Reunion

We sat talking in the summer sun,
lazing on the swing, and as it swung,
we moved from light to shadow, weaving strands
of memories and plans.
And so we added length and strength and color
from the varied fiber of our lives,
knowing that the parts may fray and ravel,
but the fabric of our family survives.

Marriage

I've been thinking about marriage lately,
not about our own because
George and I have been together
for so long
that he seems a part of me,
and I don't fuss over any part of myself
unless it's hurting.
We feel good about ourselves
and each other
and I don't know what I'd do
without him.
We agree with the same editorials
and laugh at the same jokes
and like the same people
and hold hands watching television,
which somehow gives us hope
for the future
in spite of the news.
What worries me are the divorce statistics,
the number of couples
who don't stay together long enough
to rediscover each other
after the trying years
of raising children
are over.

I worry about the Lockhorns
and the cartoons in the *New Yorker*
of the nagging wives
and grouchy husbands
in tragi-comic confrontation.
More depressing are the pictures
in small town newspapers
of Golden Anniversary couples,
those marcelled women
and tired looking men
who will stand together
in some church basement
to be congratulated on surviving.
She has long since lost her sex appeal
and settled for pats on the fanny
in the kitchen,
and he looks more interested
in cost accounting
or the back forty
than in romance.
Still, I am haunted
by the distraught old man I saw
in the corridor of the hospital
where his wife had just died.
He was leaning against the wall,
comforted by a son and a daughter,
and he said, "Please don't leave me.
I can't go home alone!"

To My Spouse

You are not my better half,
nor I, yours,
but yet a part of me,
a left hand,
(I am right handed)
which brings me the stuff of life,
holds it steady while I shape it.
I am *your* left hand,
opening doors for you to enter.
Another could not do as well,
without our shared intent
and long experience.
There is, in marriage,
an exchange of mind and muscle,
a curious balance,
often precarious,
sometimes perfect.
For forty years, we have shifted weights
as we centered into life.
I feel stronger in marriage,
than before,
and stronger each year
than the last.
Do you?

Love and Marriage

When we were young
he brought me flowers
for the prom,
small be-ribboned clusters
of sweetheart roses
and baby's breath
that wilted on my breast
in the heat of the dance,
and we called it love.

Now, each Saturday,
he comes from the Farmer's Market
with tall spears of flaming gladioli
and crusty home-made bread
and white and yellow cheeses
and shiny purple egg-plants
and ruffled green lettuce
and plump red tomatoes
and Hickory nuts
and raspberries,
even in October,
and we call it marriage.

Eye of the Beholder

"You are beautiful" he says,
and I search the mirror to see
what it is that he still finds
beautiful in me.
Moonlight
from a long-remembered shore,
goodbyes
from a long forgotten war,
mysteries,
long ago revealed,
promises,
in rapture sealed,
now fulfilled.

Delayed Reaction

Why do I see myself
in the girl on the bicycle
or the student in the classroom
or the young mother with her children,
but never in the aging woman
who stares at me so insistently
from every mirror that I pass?

Reflection

I passed a mirror recently
and saw my mother there.
She seemed surprised to see me . . .
I'd caught her unaware.
But there's no mistake about it.
The dewlaps and graying hair
are so familiar to me,
I'd know them anywhere!

Second Marriage Late In Life

No old hurts that never healed,
no angers unresolved,
no guilt and no regret.
No parents looking over our shoulders,
no children underfoot.
Just you and I together,
our aging no surprise,
friends and lovers sharing
the harvest of our lives.

Cousin Cathy, Once Removed

She lay there old, frail,
the last of her family,
with no one to care but grand nieces
and cousins once removed.
A golden sea of grain
waved in the summer sun
beyond the window of the Home.
We spoke of Willa Cather.
She was a link between
our disparate age and situation.
Through Antonia, I too had experienced
ripening wheat and changing seasons
and pioneering self-sufficiency.
Through Willa Cather and others,
she had lived
beyond the boundaries of her village
and more than her ninety years.
I marveled at her memory
and came another day to talk to her
but she was gone.
The bed was empty, bare.
No imprint of her fragile frame
remained on the smooth, cold sheet.
Still, beyond the window
waved the field of yellow grain,
soon to feel the reaper's blade,
but sure to grow again.

You Were There

We came to say goodbye
and you were there,
in the clear notes of the bells
when they were rung,
in the rafters of the church
where you had sung,
in every voice that spoke of you,
in memories they evoked of you,
you were there
in the church of our fathers
where we gathered
to celebrate your life
and lay you to rest beside them.

The Portrait

By the time I knew your mother
she was frail and bent with age.
How exciting to see her
in the portrait on your wall,
painted in the bright colors of her youth,
capturing the beauty and the spirit
of the young woman she felt herself to be
for all the days of her life.

Class Reunion

We start the day with raspberries,
extravagant pleasure
on a cold October morning.
They are full and ripe
and he says, as he tastes them,
"This is as near as I've ever been
to heaven!"
I remind him that he has often
said as much to me,
and we laugh together.
We are happier today,
having raspberries out of season
at the Union League Club in Chicago,
than we were when he was
working his way through college,
and I was worried
about the next exam,
and neither of us knew
who we were
or where we were going.

Today, we are going
to a class reunion,
to look for familiar faces
beneath the puffy eyes
and sagging cheeks
of classmates
whom we never really knew,
because forty years ago
we hardly knew ourselves.
We are all larger than life now,
with accomplishments wrapped round us
in layers,
and we display our children
and grandchildren
like jewels.
We congratulate each other
on surviving,
then return, with relief,
to the quiet of our room.
In the morning
there are raspberries again,
to savor on the long trip
home.

The Sense of Wonder

They say all things are wondrous
to a child;
I say the sense of wonder
grows with age.
The child accepts the faceless voice
that speaks through telephones,
takes moon walk in his stride,
nor doubts that man can fly
in winged machines.
He knows the sun will rise,
that spring will come
and seeds will bud and bloom,
assuming that they bear their fruit
for him.
He takes for granted fugues and virtuosos,
and counts cathedral spire
no greater than his tower of blocks,
while I watch, with awe and wonder,
the flight of a bird,
the birth of a child,
the growth of a tree,
the faith of man
that conquers pain
with hope and charity.

Each day brings new possibilities.
Each day I see further into the universe,
deeper into the heart.
Each day I discover new relationships,
between the flower and the child,
between the present and the past,
between the whole and the part,
between myself and others.
The child asks why
and then forgets to listen.
The adult listens
without knowing why.

What Is Marriage?

Marriage is
trust in each other,
faith in the future,
commitment to life.
Marriage means
that I love you
for what you are,
and I will honor you
for what you become.
In marriage
we create life
as we were created,
we nurture life
as we were nurtured,
we promise life
for generations to come.
In marriage we say,
Yes!
I do!
I will!
to *life*.

To a Son

I loved you as a baby
and I loved you as a boy,
but to know you as a man
is a special kind of joy.

Mother Love

I give you love
but do not ask it back
lest it should die with me.
It is for you to give
to spouse, to children
and to friends,
that I may see it grow
and know
that it flows endlessly
from me.

A Guest at the Wedding

Who is this man
who stands before the minister
to take his vow
of love and loyalty
to this young woman
even more unknown to me?
Surely not my son.
My son is but a boy,
hiding in the shadows
of my memory.

Yet there he stands,
strong and confident,
in every way a man.
If it is true
that all our body cells
have been replaced
each seven years,
then long ago
he shed the last of me,
cell by cell
painlessly.

No one was ever born complete.
We build upon ourselves each day
by choices that we make.
Today we come to celebrate
the choosing of a mate.

We come with gifts
of porcelain and silver,
and with our love
and hopes for them
as they move deeper
into life.

I wish for them
the comfort of the close embrace,
the joy of interests shared,
and the blessing of children,
that they may find their way
to the front row
of other weddings
in the company
of bright, resourceful,
caring men and women
who clung to them
when they were small
and who now lead them
down the aisle.

Thoughts on a Reading
at the Wedding of a Son

italics from the *Ninth Duino Elegy* of Rainer Maria Rilke

Because being here means so much . . .
> being with our children
> and their children
> on the banks of this stream
> where marigolds bloom
> and the zither plays
> and we celebrate love
> and hope
> and the promise of new life.

and because all that's here,
vanishing so quickly . . .
> as the seasons change
> and the children grow tall
> and we grow old

seems to need us
and strangely concerns us.
> Because of us
> our children are here.
> Because they are here
> our life flows on
> past folding chairs
> on a grassy slope
> in the lengthening rays
> of the summer sun.

Every Woman Knows

There is no room for Mother
when you move into his heart.
She is gently relegated
to his mind,
encased in gratitude,
but kept apart emotionally
from fear of falling
into old dependencies.
And she is happy there.
As a man, her son is strength and joy,
but she can live without him.
It is the child he was
that she carries in her heart,
and would not share with any woman,
even with his wife.

Pictures on the Wall

There stands my father,
younger than my son,
and he, the baby
in another frame,
is father now,
and I, who walk
the corridor between,
hold them both in close embrace
and they are one.

Where Did All My Children Go?

I nursed them and changed them
and rocked them to sleep,
I sang to them and read to them
and held them close,
never knowing I could let them go.

Now grown men and women
come bearing gifts for Mother's Day.
I'm proud of them and love them all,
but sometimes I dream
of the children they were,
so dear to me,
now lost to me forever.

When You Come For a Visit

When you come for a visit
you fit so naturally into your place
in our hearts and in our lives
that it seems you've never been away.
Having you near reaffirms our connection
and we hold you close.

When you leave there are no tears.
You are free to go your way
to be what you can be,
and we are free to stay in place
secure in what we've come to be.

The Grandmother

She comes to celebrate another birth
to cook and clean and rock the baby
while the mother sleeps.
She stays until the parents know
that with the child
comes milk enough to nourish
and instincts they can trust.
And when she leaves she tells them
what she has learned from mothering . . .
you never regret
any loving you give them.

To Grown Children Bearing Gifts

There is no need for flowers
in profusion,
nor words of praise
beyond what I have earned.
Just honor me for some small thing
that I did well,
forgive me for some flaw,
and if you must bring offering
a single rose would say it all.
You are the gift.
You are the celebration.
I could not ask for more.

Celebration

We gather round the table
to celebrate another birthday.
It is her grandmother's table,
transported across the country
to this new home of hers.
We could be thousands of miles
and generations away,
so much it evokes
of birthdays past.
Only the faces change.
Her children light the candles now,
and proudly bear the cake.
Her husband sits at the head of the table
as we, her parents, newly grand,
move aside to celebrate
on-going life.

To a Grandchild

Thank you for looking like your mother,
for giving us a hand to hold
and a child to hug,
when we thought she'd grown
away from us.
You are our seed,
and your blossoming keeps us growing
into the future.

Thank you for being your own person,
and for bringing your father's genes
into our family
to enrich us with new strengths
and possibilities.

Thank you for your laughter,
which is contagious,
and for your tears,
which show us that you care.
Is it any wonder that we love you?

A Visit to Grandmother

When you come, her arms will reach out
to hold you close for a while.
She will have made up your father's bed for you,
and brought out the old worn blocks.
She will play Animal Lotto with you,
and read Ferdinand and Winnie the Pooh.
And when you go, she will cry
because she knows the child she loves
will never come again.
Another year and he will have grown
further into the man he is to be,
and though she will love him more,
today she is bereaved.

Peanut Butter and Jelly

The grandchildren are gone
and I am left
with unmade beds
and wet towels
and odd sox
and peanut butter and jelly
on the living room rug
and bare spots on the lawn
(to mark the bases)
and an empty place in my heart
and an unholy glee
in being free again
to be me.

There Is No Middle Age

There is no middle age.
You're either old or you are young.
You say, "Yes, sir!" for half your life,
while climbing, rung by rung
up the ladder of success,
but when you reach the top,
you're done!

You're the newest of vice-presidents,
with a carpet on the floor,
but before your job is done,
another name is on your door.

You're the young one on committees,
half afraid to speak your mind,
then you're chairman ex-officio,
with duties left behind.

You learn to raise your children
by the time they've gone from home.
When you have the time and money,
you no longer care to roam.

You exercise your muscles
just to feel them turn to putty.
You try to come off witty
and you end up sounding nutty.

You're too liberal for your father
and too stodgy for your son.
You've debated all the issues
but you feel you've never won.

You spend a lifetime learning.
Do you then become a sage?
You never know how little you know
'til you're well past middle age.

The Kinship of Women

We find it when we talk among ourselves
    of love and marriage,
    of giving birth,
    of raising children,
    and letting go.

We feel it when we share
    our joys and sorrows,
    our hopes and fears,
    our angers and frustration.

We know it when we come together
    for work or play
    and find strength and courage
    in each other.

The kinship of women
    is an abiding,
    renewable,
    life-affirming blessing.

Perception

Her face lights with a smile
when we meet unexpectedly
on the streets of our town.
She is my child, grown tall,
with interests and a family
of her own.
We meet as adults,
accepting our sameness,
celebrating our difference,
seeing each other in new ways
now that she is mother too.
But no amount of love and respect
can change our relationship.
She must see in me the profile of her aging
and her death.
I see in her the promise
of immortality.

The Druggist Likes Me As I Am

My blood is laced with cortisone,
my heart is fibrillating,
my bones are losing calcium,
my muscles, stiff and aching.
My teeth are full of cavities,
my stomach's gone to pot,
my heartburn interferes with sleep,
my energy is shot.
My hair is getting grayer,
my eyes are growing dim;
if I don't control my moustache
I'll be taken for a him.
With all the subterfuge required,
the costly reconstruction,
is there anything about me
that is safe from this destruction?
The running down, the wearing out
is there for all to see
and I have to fight it daily,
but it isn't really me.
That's in my poetry.

CAT Scan

I lie motionless on the metal cart
that glides slowly, majestically,
into the awesome other-world
of the X-ray machine.
I breathe and stop breathing
in response to the muffled voice
of an attendant carefully shielded
from the rays that bombard me.
They penetrate my body
to uncover my darkest secrets,
lesions that could destroy me.
I am quiet, hoping to escape the truth.

In the room across the hall,
a young couple waits
for word from the doctor.
"It is twins!" he says.
The young woman catches her breath
then laughs.
She cannot stop laughing
and her happiness flows down the corridor,
touching everyone.
I think of the changes in their life,
and in ours,
and I cannot grieve.
Their joy is contagious
and I laugh with them.

The Hospital

The door opens
without my touch,
and closes automatically
against the world.
I am assigned to a cubicle
by computer,
stripped of my identity
along with my clothes,
and reduced to a set of statistics
on a chart.
My will is taken away,
with my money and my rings,
for my own protection.
My pride is stored
in a plastic cup
with my removable bridge.

My mind and my heart
become less interesting
than blood and urine.
Within hours, I will be drugged
and assaulted
by masked strangers with knives
who will determine my future
while I sleep.
Ye god-like monitors
of my heartbeat
and my aspiration,
don't mistake me
for the bloody sheets
you change routinely
and throw aside so carelessly
to be sanitized
and bleached!

When I Am Old

When I am old,
don't look down on me,
for I have stood tall.
Don't speak for me;
I have not lost my will.
Don't talk behind my back;
I hear more than you know.
Don't laugh at this old flesh;
there is a young spirit inside.
Be patient while I move aside
for you to rush by.
Keep your balance
lest *you* fall
before your time.

Glory Be!

I am eighty years old and happier
than I have ever been in my life!

I have found excitement in love
and fulfillment in marriage.

I have felt life stirring in my womb
and rejoiced in the birth of children.
I have lived to marvel at their growth,
their talents, and their children.

I have found my voice . . .
written down my thoughts and feelings,
and shared them with others
who have found themselves
in the pages of my books.

I live among kindred spirits . . .
friends who will share an idea
or lend a helping hand;
people who accept their limitations
with grace and humor
and celebrate each day as it comes.

I have lived and loved
beyond my expectations.

Glory be!

A Last Letter to My Spouse

This morning I drank from your empty cup.
It is only days since you left us
so abruptly that we cannot believe you are gone.
Death is so hard to accept that I still feel
you are behind the closed door of an unknown room,
or away on an unexpected trip and will surely return.

It will take time for me to realize
that you will never again
   sleep in my bed,
   sit at my table,
   or share my thoughts and feelings.

I miss you in increments:
   in the suits that hang lifeless in your closet,
   in the shaving lotion you have used
   since we were courting,
   in the grocery store
   where I walk past your favorite foods,
   in the unopened *Wall Street Journal*,
   in the shut down computer,
   in the piano you will never play again,
   in the letters from friends remembering you
   for your competence, your intelligence,
   your kindness and your wit.

You stood tall beside me
for all of our years together
and you stood firm behind our children
while we grew into a family.
You questioned our rash statements
and challenged our assumptions
but we never doubted that you loved us.
Thank you for trusting our judgment
and for supporting us in every way.
You made us strong.

You have gone to your rest
leaving something of yourself in each of us.
We love you and miss you.
We will honor you with our lives.

G.

Survival

We were laughing and talking
when his heart stopped beating . . .
but the body they carried away on the gurney
was not the man I married.
He is still with me.

I see him in the face and form of our children
and hear him in their voices.
I find him in the kind words
of those who knew him,
and hear him in his own words
as I speak them.
I know how he would feel
about the editorials in the *Times*
and that he would like our new neighbors,
and why.
There is no need for further conversation.
In our years together
we have said it all.

Thoughout our marriage
when he traveled
I found I could live without him
because our love and trust were strong.
Even when he was on a minesweeper in the Pacific
I felt him near me and could cope.

Now I know that we survive
without our loved ones
because they are forever a part of us.
We learn through loss
that when our life is over,
more lives on than dies with us.

Eternity Enow

We learn from loss
that death is not the end of life:
We continue to grow
in the seeds we've sown
    in our gardens,
    in our work,
    in our children
    and our friends.
The spirit that lives on
is not illusion.
It is the vital energy
that strengthens all
whose lives we've touched.

Eternity enow.

Flowers for the Living

"Flowers for the living" he would say
of a kind word or an unexpected gift
to a loved one or a friend.

When he died, I could not cry for him.
His was a long life, well lived
and he was free at last
of weakness and of pain.
At his service we celebrated his strengths
and counted our blessings.

But on his birthday there were tears.
I wanted to thank him again
for the years of love and companionship we shared
and for the gift of life he gave to me
in our children.
There would be no celebration this year,
no cake or burning candles.
A light and some of sweetness
had gone from my life.

Then came flowers with a card saying:
"Flowers for the living. Love, Dave."
There was resurrection and immortality
in the kindness of our son
and I felt anew the healing power of love.

If I Were Young Again

If I were young again
I'd wear white dimity and lace,
and flowers in my hair.
I'd swim naked in the moonlight
and make love on mossy rocks
beside the sea.
I'd sing and dance
and try to capture on my canvas
sun refracted from the leaves of trees.

I was old when I was young,
trying to probe the mystery
of life and death.
Now I know that they endure
without my knowledge or consent.
Death is unseen, unfelt,
of passing interest
to him who carves our name
and final date on stone.
Life is our response,
to sights and sounds,
to words of truth,
to acts of love.
All else is postscript,
even poetry.

The Berkshires

Gentle rolling hills,
no jagged peaks,
no deep gorges,
their height nonthreatening,
their valleys protective,
their presence reassuring.
They are worn down by time
but not worn away.
So it seems to be with me.

Melon Seed

The seeds of the melon,
in their multiplicity,
and the acorns on the oak
that could each become a tree,
are my best hope
for life on earth
in perpetuity.

So Let It Be

Let me die peacefully
in my own bed,
when work is done
and children raised
and my full share
of tears and laughter
spent.
The accident,
the fiery death
are an abbreviation.
I want to write
The End to life,
though hand grows weak
and letters dim.

I have watched the old die.
There comes a time when,
face to wall
and food untouched,
they choose to sleep.
So let it be
with me.

When I Die

When I die,
don't put a stone on me
and leave me alone
with strangers.
Take me to the village
where my father was born,
to the church yard
where he and my mother lie buried,
and where all the tombstones
are of family and friends.
Scatter my ashes
on our common ground
and plant a tree nearby,
that I may nourish roots
and keep on growing.

To Die in Peace

When I die, don't cry for me.
My time will come and I am at peace,
knowing that the things that mean the most to me
live on.

My children and their children
will keep me alive in their memory
and will carry me with them into the future.

The sun will rise each day without me,
the seasons will come and go
and all things living will grow
in their predestined way
to blossom, bear their fruit and die.
Their seeds will take root in new soil.

Every generation,
in its own time and its own way
will build and restore,
will invent and explore,
will read and write,
will dance and sing,
will laugh and cry.

Lovers will cling to each other
and mothers will hold their babies close.
With each touch,
with each hug,
with each hand clasped,
with each kind word,
love and fellowship will be renewed.
This is what we learn with age.
This is why we die in peace.

Is it so small a thing
To have enjoyed the sun,
To have lived light in the spring,
To have loved, to have thought, to have done?

From *The Hymn of Empedocles*, Matthew Arnold

Index

*From *Queen Anne's Lace,* 1982.
† From *The Sound of the Harp,* 1989.

Remember me is all I ask,
and if remembering be a task,
forget me.

Unknown